The
Water Books

poems by
Judith Vollmer

The Water Books

poems by

Judith Vollmer

Autumn House Press • Pittsburgh, Pennsylvania

Autumn House Press Staff
Editor-in-Chief and Founder: Michael Simms
Co-Founder: Eva-Maria Simms
Community Outreach Director: Michael Wurster
Managing Editor: Adrienne Block
Fiction Editors: Sharon Dilworth, John Fried
Associate Editors: Ziggy Edwards, Erik Rosen, Rebecca King
Assistant Editor: D. Gilson
Media Consultant: Jan Beatty
Publishing Consultant: Peter Oresick
Technology Consultant: Evan Oare
Tech Crew Chief: Michael Milberger
Intern: Caroline Tanski

 PENNSYLVANIA COUNCIL ON THE ARTS Autumn House Press receives state arts funding support through a grant from the Pennsylvania Council on the Arts, a state agency funded by the Commonwealth of Pennsylvania, and the National Endowment for the Arts, a federal agency.

ISBN: 978-1-932870-54-1

Library of Congress Control Number: 2011909817

for

Patricia Dobler (1939-2004)

and

Peter Oresick

Acknowledgments

Thanks to the editors of the following publications in which these poems—some in different versions—have appeared or are about to:

Agni: "Kinzua"

Along These Rivers, Poetry and Photography from Pittsburgh: "Field Near Rzeszow"

Cerise Press: "Birds of Rome"

The Fourth River: "Trees at Night," "Cleaning the Alley," "Camping on the Hudson"

The Gettysburg Review: "Far from Home I Consider the Body & the Engine"

The Great River Review: "I Take My Mother to See the Rothko Panels, 2007," "My Orange," "Skyline & Sky"

Natural Language: An Anthology of Poetry Celebrating the Carnegie Library Reading Series: "To a Lamp"

New South: "New Black Dress"

Poet Lore: "January Work"

Poetry International: "Hole in the Sky"

Thanks to the American Academy in Rome and the Corporation of Yaddo for solitude during which many of these poems were drafted or completed. Thanks are also due to the University of Pittsburgh at Greensburg, friends in the Pittsburgh poetry community, and the poets of the Drew University MFA Program in Poetry and Poetry in Translation, especially Michael Waters, Mihaela Moscaliuc, Anne Marie Macari, and Gerald Stern.

My heartfelt gratitude for ongoing support goes to Maggie Anderson, Jan Beatty, Lynn Emanuel, Lori Jakiela, Dave Newman, Ed Ochester, Mary Taylor Simeti, Ron Wallace, Michael Wurster; and, most of all, Ann Begler.

Finally, thank you to the Autumn House Press staff, particularly Michael Simms.

Table of Contents

I. New Black Dress

II. My Orange
Giovanni Pascoli *November* (from the Italian)

III. Kinzua
Giovanni Pascoli *Night Jasmine* (from the Italian)

IV. In an Ancient Garden
Giacomo Leopardi
from *To the Broom Flowers of Pompeii* (from the Italian)

The Water Books

I.
New Black Dress

New Black Dress

I slip it over my head & step out into dusk

softest time on the planet, feel its weight & folds

Streetlamps are turning themselves on

like relaxed insomniacs

& evening releases its green sugar & white oils

Glide the car onto the Boulevard of the Allies & admire

the windows silver-foiling their reflections of the Hot Metal Bridge

Would it be nice   to go from youth straight to death

no thin hair   loose teeth   no mind-slipping   just the ragbin

What's possible   pleasure of a simple dress

neckline to hem

the body of the shift

floating above the shift-gears of the nightrivers

where otters slide onto their backs

in the deep Monongahela again

their eyelashes filtering silt from liquid   near from far

maybe a keyhole view of a deep black dress

holding another creature also

silk & fur & bone

Could I wear this dress till its cottonsilk

grows into my skin   corpse dress

its fine cinder-black ground to ash

Pack light   move on

with all who travel by river or sea

What's possible   latitudes—Pittsburgh:

40 degrees, Rome: 41—not so far-off

if parallel lines meet in space   but I miss my new friends

& won't see them for two years

Their gift of a dress

folded into a paper sleeve & mailed

from Monteverde in time for

now   Tonight belongs to her new moon body

with its translucent hem running

the circumference of its black rhinestone tail

Field Near Rzeszow

—family field in the Carpathians originally passed down through
the line of women

> *How I had thought*
> *this field, that meadow*
>
> *is branded for eternity—*
> H.D., "R.A.F." 1941

If these young rye flowers
stand up every summer
then fall under grindstones
& fists of bakers,

if the stalks return to earth, rough,
& return green every Spring,
    and if the ditches the aircraft wheels made

exist only in a censored photograph
    and in grass-tracings above tiny black *allées*
        down where worms make their tracks

why am I standing on an open balcony
dreaming for my own land,
    & hers before me?

                    Two men play guitars
down in the street on the edge of town
    and sing about the sky—
                    say, then shout, *niebo*
in a high laughing song, then

7

a woman's voice interrupts, in English,
    I see the back of her head
    which looks tired, but she sounds intent,
    we are all shouting

    and I wish I knew Polish well enough
    to hear the song again,

backstitch whose sky
        whose field, and who owns
the fernbanks across the field.

If I really owned this land
I would like to lie down on it through thirty seasons.

      Go into the woods
      get the black dirt
      for the flower pots

      Save the brown water
      from the sinks & tubs,
      save the dregs of the soup pot
      for the geraniums,
      save the coffee grounds for the roses.

      Dig for the best nightcrawlers
      under the shadows of boulders
      at the edge of the meadow where the table-
      rock piled with the big rocks
      writes its story in long lines—

I would do these things.
I would study the scars
& glyphs the moraines clawed
in granite & limestone when the mammoth
plates scraped the land. When they stopped
moving they left overhangs & ledges,

& rock-niches for succulents & rock-rose.
        I get the hair-on-the-back-of-the-neck sensation
    at the edge of a field
        and like to read
    in the grass of a ditch
where weeds show
      spitpockets inside their blades,
  and the thatchings give groundcover
    to pebbles usually brown & black & sometimes a white
quartz fragment sits there reflecting
    light up into the bird & butterfly paths.

Snakes, insect clouds & rabbits
  must like the heat of earth at that
        close range. And the tall blue

flowers rimming the deer beds—
        like hairlines.
Don't
    work late,
        the field spirits come out at dusk—
        Night lasts all night.

Not much to go on, my field's war-time biography—
the photo:
a simple field stolen x times over.
Unseal it and see:

the original wedding gift,
the furrows turned,
moist, open.

One word, *niebo*,
translates part of the song:

If I say I like your *niebieska* blouse
I mean *blue*.
        When I say
the only *niebo* for me
is the one above my family field
I am calling it heaven.

On the Tarmac at Dover Air Force Base, 2006

> — *The 18-year ban on media coverage of returning American war*
> *dead was lifted in 2009.*

The sodium vapor lights look down
inside their columns of rain
and light the hot pavement sending its
steam back up. Drops of oil & rain
                    smeared by a truck, drops the size of dimes,
me looking for something
to focus on: a feather, a shoelace tip,
a comb, a rusting
       stencil I find in a storm ditch:
                      1 2 3 ZERO—
an honor guard—
       Rain eyes—
       cameras.

Under the scrims of grease, in rainwater
       you might catch a glimpse of something
              human, or mechanical,
simple acts of love and
friendship seeing the dead
on a daily basis
in their transport.

Our tongue
& soil
twist themselves in a lost key,
       the dark & the quiet are going to have to be enough
       space for thinking.

I had to sit
out under the stars last night: accidental lock-out
on my porch looking in, and I prepared
to come here and see the runway, the hangar,
all the empty parking spaces where TV trucks
should be. I lost
my key, I'd left the news on,
the windows were sealed & shining,
the evening star was blinking,
the dead show up no matter what; in the cemetery
at Frick Park you can look inside the little
houses even the rich don't visit, leaves & webs
unswept, the Tiffany glass unpolished, and down the hill
endless rows of stones
          another on another in a crooked wedding
          cake of white stones high as rowhouses,
black stones patinaed with soot & benzene, photos
of the dead under glass.

Milosz said we can't have Earth, can't
even attain it in our dreams;
what harm in coming here
seeing how & who we kill? I can't
give anything but memory,

only the eyes
might see through
the cinder layer
    the clay level—
        the mineral kingdom
        upside down.
Only the living
come to pick up their young
coffins.
    Here's a leaf: almond shaped
with water droplets, bronze leaf rinsed & leathery.

Stomping in creeks—
　　　some of the boys did that—
and the girls, some made dishes from catalpa leaves
　　　and served flower meals on them, and washed their hands
with leaves, after feeding their doll families.
The thought of boots in creekbeds
& leaf-picnics & water
　　　　　　　taking the crisp top layer of the leaf
softening it,

the thought of boot leather softened by rain, scratched by mud.

Here on asphalt having no one to greet,
and having no one to bury, bless my luck in this hour.
The dead soften inside the coffins
under the medals & the censored grief.

Cleaning the Alley

Up early & feeling long-stemmed
& moist, bright & eloquent even, a woodland pool,
I go down anyway, tie the bandana, down

the 6 steps to the margin of my sixteenth-acre
pig-eared to the alley whose blonde bricks remain the pride
of Regent Square's belle époque

when every house stocked caves of coal & ice.
Elephant ears I bow to you & attack
the mile-a-minute vine the city is burning out of the parks, here

the clutch of sumac I'll need the cudgel for. The worst
I kneel to with gloves & my old plastic windshield scraper:
the slimed untouchables: condomtwinkiedogshitbirdpart

& a fresh Skoal can dropped accidentally maybe
by the garbagemen I've been embarrassed to be seen by,
putting this off all Spring. Haywire cracks form

Pennsylvania twisted sideways
& strangely inspire me though the weeds are tight as burlap
and require the knife. I'm sweating breathing

bargrease & diesel & sucking lungfuls of heavy-
metal dust, get more bags, a bucket of water. I pull weeds knowing
labor I was intended for. Paul, our family's youngest 73-year-old

laughed the month he died: "Your problem is you're still waiting
around for the next revolution of the Left. You missed it, kid,
it was Roosevelt." I'm into this, I tend my place the way he

14

shoveled township paperwork, though he should have been Governor.
All involves mind calloused to a blunt-force tool.
I hear the mega-bus voicebox murmur "Downtown" & "Waterfront"

& feel the itchy new money drilling our Marcellus.
No future till it's made, but 50 years
without pruning and NYC would be parkland.

My state could reclaim its sylvan kingdom. This could be
wetland drinking from the city culverts & ditches.
Now the goldenrod monsters give way & fill another bag,

it's time to pour vinegar water over my 10 x 8 brick wedge:
Welcome to my house: back entrance—
the dead-headed geraniums pungent & refreshed.

Georges de Beauvoir Breaks His Silence

"Simone
has a man's brain;
she thinks like a man;
she *is* a man."

He said this without affect or inflection.
His daughter continued writing in her notebook.

Money Comes from Four Places

You steal it, twitchy fingers,
from your poor sick mother who doesn't
know a check from a book,
a ditch your mind
digs faster than the speed of the
light touch you've got there.

It's given to you:
Aruba, Tortuga, Beluga,
how many ways
can you spend it?

You earn it
by working
and it drains
itself week by week,
or you save
and enter a kingdom of virtue.

You find it as in:
a scirocco lifted it and set it down under your nose
the day you pocketed that roll of 50s you found
under the thruway.

3 dimensions
4 places
money comes from.

Whose portrait's on the C note,
whose the grand?

To a Lamp

Little moon on a silver pole
no rock will smash you on my watch

no ghost-whistle from the sad streets
of Trafford Westinghouse will scold *Go home*

no profit-siren yowl *Hurry, before you lose*
all the hours you owe us

I love your single eye-
globe of filaments

lighting the cross-hatched shrubs
& gate-posts welded at their notches

Only you, satin crookneck
brighten the ochre bricks made of clay

dug from the riverbanks
When the ambulance comes to take him

I'll have to turn back
and find my way past windows

splintering light into rings & chains
along the sidewalk between night's

floor & ceiling where this new
grieving absorbs & stores me

under the gentle attendance
of your illumination

A Woman I Meet Translates a Line from Ritsos

"These red spots on the walls could also be blood—"
—Yannis Ritsos, "The Blackened Pot"

"Not a spot on the wall as your English says   not a blotch or a smear or even
a pool of blood attached to the wall like a hardened splash, but a kind of

tattoo on the firing squad wall   flesh blasted onto the white-washed wall
a tattoo the people bear for generations   a pierced graft people see on each

other's backs as they sit on beaches of the Aegean or under olive trees   invisible
needles pick at the brand in the skin   tissue over the heart"

Sticks Found in a Ravine

Kindling, a bonfire in honor of Pasolini

who prayed to his own mother, cursing & thanking her for too much love.

His film critiques gave me a headache but his

Decamerone changed my girl-life, seeing the lover cup her hand on her man's

cock, both sleeping on an open porch.

Up here in the Pamphilii woods I'm leaving a hobo prayer stick for Pasolini, &

one for Jimmo, destroyed in the first wave of AIDS. I can never find Pasolini,

but the *Roman Poems* helped my first efforts. They do now.

It was my mother's love

let me slide my tongue inside the slit of a woman. Suck a man clean.

I can't find you in Via Carini's sweet queer *passeggiata*.

Didn't find you among Testaccio's crushed lamps & bones.

In your time

boys run to you for bags of oranges & bread.

Boys you run to for love, and vanish in smoke & hunger.

A few of these words sting with sweet salt

from this gay life neither you nor I

fully embrace.

Say the body beautiful *wherever it falls on the slippery continuum,*

you wrote. Your Friulian, your local-rough dialect

busted the Italian canon wide open.

You shouldn't have gone after desperate boys with guns at night.

Were you

meeting your beloved, do you,

does anybody

know what really happened?

Dear famous lovechild.

Skyline & Sky

Thanks to the cattail rain
the terra cotta pots are saturating
& their salt essences will patina
offering new maps to think about.
The ant colonies must be in their sand hills
the jays in their white pine
waiting out this easy, straight-down shower
that pounds the straw under the Italian
parsley & flashes the canoe-shaped sage leaves
green then silver. Rain is
soaking the cattynines fleshier
& the height they project sharpens my
comprehension of skyline & sky
in front of me the delicate ladder
of the clematis, & the sideways scribbles of
Jasper Johns whose book I'm reading
on my porch. He called it scribbling
but could do it in his sleep, he could
make a line twist & release a wash
thick or thin not only at the edges but inside the wild
lakes of his blues, marking depths &
miniature Gulf Streams. I imagine him
thinking then sketching time
itself as it occurs in the making of
a cattail reed, the tall entity it becomes,
damp & thinly fibrous at first
then darker as its fur-velvet accumulates
up from stem to tip. Every mark of his pen
darkens the empty space, but holes
remain, rifts, so that during a summer rain

an entire population of gnats might take shelter
in a single cattail,
free space, pinprick of habitat,
their nonstop breathing factory
of eyes, lenses, rods & cones
in their haven & 12-hour lives.

II.
My Orange

GIOVANNI PASCOLI

November

Jewel-air, sun so clear
you look for apricots
blossoming, and your heart
smells the bitterish hawthorne.

But the tree's dry
and plant-like sticks mark the sky
with black designs.
The galaxy's empty,
the earth feels hollow,
echoes under my boots.

Silence all around: but in the wind,
pacing, you hear the distances
from orchards & gardens,
brittle leaves falling.
It's cold. For the dead, it's summer.

My Orange

Take one
from the basket
with the cup of bittersweet coffee, this is all
I'm going to get this morning because
Vittorini is teaching me again another membrane

of truth so do not repeat
my spendthrift days, the ones that went
uneaten, little suns on my bookshelf
dried up pulp & laces.
Now when I try for greater focus
every plate means something & yes there's no
food in *The Charterhouse of Parma* because Stendhal was obese
& maybe punishing himself & now there's another new war
& time is so tight. Now bend my thumb

angle it down through the oily skin
of the globe, thank
the old cast-offs
tucked into the toes of the Christmas stockings
(I was digging for Kennedy halves
& the walnuts & chocolates). In the lunch box
I wanted concentrate
or the horrible Tang
the astronauts packed into space—Though we're known

throughout the world
for our bombs,
our baskets glow with the light
of a thousand miles of trees

& the human
fingers of the pickers
burnt with the sweet acid.

Birds of Rome

That crow guaranteed my entrance to the cult of grappa
at the bar in Monteverde where my heartache weighted
the floorboards. This one will pick the lock on my desk
where someone carved *Beware all who enter—*. I love the Roman
day that feels like 2, invite the swallow to follow me to my neighbor
child, Bruno, 8, while he conducts the doves: "LOUDER!"
as they finish sipping Campari droplets from the ATM gutter
while I lean over my window-box letting flowerwater drip down 2
stories. I've leaned all Spring beside the lemons and fallen asleep
on my huge pink desk, I tilt lowdown to the river gods' invisible arms.
When I was a girl in Rome, you could smell the woods inside the
alcoves; I offered crumbs & straws to the laborers weaving nests into the
Janiculum and sat on a bench before the *viale rustica* waiting
with secrets & shadows.
 Now sun-shards blink off cane & stroller handles,
& pods sweating money. *Stop interrupting me*, street of green windows,
I've sketched you. I circle the Pantheon twice, take my seat, wait, 8 a.m., chilled,
sweaterless, sipping from a cup with a lion's face. Now the firemen
scale the dome and reach the oculus with sacks of rose petals they will
drop down through the eye: Pentecost.
 I forget the blood-popes & gold-
mongers, it's possible to fall in love with a building, as I have
among the pilgrims. I enter the vestibule, celebrating the lamb's
sharp hoofs. "The ocean is so big, how will we get over it?" I asked
my father. "There is a huge tall bridge and we will walk right across it,"
he said, daydreaming, thinking I was afraid. I was learning to read, &
memorizing people as birds. He was a swivel-brained owl, my brothers
were bald eaglets, mother a swan splaying her daily costume. I was a head
w/glasses, question-mark. Now the river's green lungs lift with herons.
Sheets of light peel off the waters. A surge lifts a fountain of Aquafina bottles.
Two gulls touch down to the silver knives of their nestlings' open beaks.

28

When, on a Late March Evening

I catch the vision of fingerless gloves on the bus stop girl with scarlet nails, she looks flat so I greet the sidewalk, turn onto my block and see the hooded guy perched on the corner who tried living in our roofless garage one winter; I dialed, a young cop seemed sad when he said, "He said you said he could stay here." Now he's older and looks like the Unabomber one of my students believed was a contemporary version of Thoreau and he waves a crooked hi to me from behind his scarf. I don't wave back but remember the political theory prof who said we quickly submit when the government knocks on the door and seduces our kids to wars, but if it took our cars we would take to the streets. Sick of fear I eat & preen, whisper to my dead who made me when they were young and taught me to keep a wish even a mini-vision going under the drum-tight clock tower.

A Reckoning

— *following the canned hunts at Rolling Rock Club,*
Ligonier, Pennsylvania, 2003, 2007

— "*Doing canned hunting is like*
having sex with a blow-up doll."
—*local hunter, Western Pennsylvania*

When Cheney's men pushed the 500
out of their pens & downhill
toward the hidden blinds   pushed the ring-necks

they "flew" never having "flown" before
all having been fitted with goggles
Some were kicked

until they opened their wings & lifted
off the grass & "flew" downward
The 500 lifting into darkness

wearing goggles not so they
wouldn't see death   but so
they wouldn't see well enough to catch-

or-sense a current and lift into the far
        Pheasants, your neck-rings picked
up the sun-glints too, your feet bent back

into flight position, flexing, aerodynamic,
the extended **Y** shapes did exactly
what they're designed to do, to lift off

in short brilliant flight
    Your double-sheened fluorescence—

Your colors gleamed exactly the way
they're designed to do:
Light sliding from the East

satins your cobalt with malachite.
Light sliding from the West
makes a simpler greenblack, tinged with purple—

Fitted with goggles
not so you wouldn't see
death, but so you wouldn't fly into the far

woods of the 10,000 acres
of Rolling Rock Farm maintained by Mellon
offspring & The Heritage Foundation

Rocks that form the mountains
who take their name
from the fringes of wild laurel

Dense, accordioned rockmass
Spruce so thick
the waters filtering down through the rock-

folds remain the purest in the Mid Atlantic
Dick Cheney having shot 70 ring-necks &
three dozen mallards himself

Antonin Scalia   number unknown
Rick Santorum   shaking hands   No blood

The pheasants "cleaned, packed, & sent
to those less fortunate"

No comment No record
to which soup kitchens or shelters
the 500 traveled

Boys like Cheney trap frogs
& stuff two or three firecrackers down
their throats, and watch them blow to smithereens

mid-air. Party of 10 stand sipping
their drinks   Wait for the click of the gate
& the rush of birds in the jerky release

throttling downhill   Time it—
goggles speeding past
O great black mask of death

monsters
little forevers
beautiful brief flight

Kitchen Apologia

A half-circle of steaming dishes
& first spring lettuces
ready for the table

where we wept & wailed.
If I could grind a concentrate
of the last X years,

name that enormous space
I'd make it bittersweet, as usual,
but make sure the oil

is so green & fragrant it lifts
a golden cloud before your face—
make a wish—then walk

into the heart of an orchard,
birds & sunbursts dervishing around our heads
& horseshoes clanking in the grass,

every single hurt dissolving
under the earth's calendar & how
we nearly
broke each other.

To an Aide at Shift-Change

I see
    you're left-handed
        & I want to be reading
Leonardo's notebooks while eating licorice.
I see your slashed jeans & fingerless gloves, fresh
date-gear after the filthy scrubs & quick shower.
I see your name tag, Crystal,
tucked into your flowered tote.
              I lose myself
in your sweater's blue weave, I'm salt-
pitted, already stone
here in the sitting chair
while my mother nods off, freshly bathed

by you who are threading yourself out of
the smells & cries, chatting,
praising when she said
"I picked up my shoes,
they were interrupting the floor"

the treadmill you step off now
"Outta here," your plucked-to-gone
eyebrows & thin hair, yellow
fingertips & skinny wrists,
your turn into the line
between midnight & night
fusing me to the chair.

34

The Letters

The lists the lies
the facts
those I burned
in an April
apartment white on white

I burned them in broad daylight
in a small brass bowl
laments & obstacles scrawled
on folded paper-bits

those I calmly burned
they curled
in hoops & wheels
that climbed walls

their shadows crawled
the wallboards, I stared them
down to shreds
I stared myself to sleep

      The letters remain
unsorted & languorous
among linens & candles
tidepools & openair desks

unsorted in their
sealed room, so
I don't feel

their creases & fine bond
or see the hand

the ink the intimate
imprint of your expressions

Hole in the Sky

The dead ascend to heaven through white holes
into blue and that is why The Virgin's robe
was blue, the priestdrone easy to believe until
she died
who fed & combed me
with the callused palm of her hand. When she died
I hid under the cellar steps
shredding the hem of my skirt,
it calmed me to see colors in the weave.
The sky sucked her up, Reverse Hell, it was icy
& lonely and the sucking tornado hole of it
took her from the other hole
no one stayed to see the dirt packed onto.
I was going up through the hole
I thought, sitting under the steps
& ceiling vents with all the other
houses along the old boulevards & alleybacks
facing the yellow rivers
and the huge rushes & mists furled
upward, escapes always up into the sky. I look
up and she's still alive to me
but not her
human world of steel buckets & sour boots & septic
fractures in the foundations & men
blowing their noses into their fingers.

Trees at Night

Until the storm arrives from Chicago they will rock or sway
their uppermost stick-bundles & leaf-crowns,

buffet the jay fledglings in their straw & twine-bit
nest, then settle them back down, then take a quick breather or two

until they restart the tipping & the rustling
whose sound if properly recorded would be soft as dust

under the nets of lightly scattered star-cover
Their graceful fans lave the pavement & sift astringents onto

the strata of fryer grease & bar smoke, sewer acid,
gathering, anointing themselves, flexible leaf-skins

pliable stems veined chlorophyll channels processing rain mist fog snow-
ghosts & sound-memories of hail pellets & wind squalls   Branches work

their genius of variation, no dip or arc repeating any other
no particle of reflection too small to miss the dance upon railings

& bumpers, eyeglasses & bottle shards, lamp-steel, mailbox
handle, & human eye-white all under the spell of the late October New Moon.

Far from Home I Consider the Body & the Engine

When they got a little older my nephews asked me

Did you know Jurgen Vollmer invented the Beatles' haircut? Is he our uncle?
Can you get a girl pregnant the first time?
How many universes do you think there are?
Why don't you quit your job & travel around for five years?

When we visited the Museum of Flight they taught me
if you have to you can fly across the United States
on a plane made of two aluminum panels, the movement
of your own body, & a small engine you can
cut or start as needed.

Entering

--for Vera, in search of the sheela-nagig (ancient Irish vulva) in Rome

I feel the curvature, but barely;
entering the city on stone cold radials
           that stretch & extend themselves
       out from the cervix of the center
       among thousands of centers, I look up

high along a balustrade the ancient carved almond, *mandorla,*
the almond-slit, *vesica piscis,*
       the death-woman opens her legs & holds,

so all see while they're walking & looking up
the open muscles & lips
casting (what?)

down on smartcars, buses, bikes, carts, wheelbarrows
the swollen massive rosettes of the birther-to-all-men
lifecunt dripping onto
streetcars' silver-hot tracks—

Once young women squatted over the open furrows:
          bountiful harvest

My own yoni heart
    sheening itself with so much touching:
   moist tentacles of the vicoli I twist inside of

I nod to the old woman almond
    crumbling;

above, a fresh tag:
    Stop beating women

This walk my feet were made for:
    the flight, bag, coat I dropped
        coming back to the Via Giulia

on a Monday morning in May
        moving past the excavations &
displays of the dead

III.
Kinzua

GIOVANNI PASCOLI

Night Jasmine

Night flowers open the hours
I think of those I love.
The dusk butterflies arrived at the viburnums,
the crying stopped a while ago.
Across the street a house settles.
Nests relax under wings
like eyes under lids.
The scent of ripe strawberries
lifts from open goblets.
A lamp shines in my front room.
Grass springs from ditches.
A late bee hums: the cells
are already taken.
A hen struts the blue-ing yard
followed by her starry chirping.

All night long
scent passes with the wind.
Light drifts up the stairs: glows
out from the first floor: is shut off.
Now it's dawn and jasmine petals
close, slightly crumpled.
In those soft secret urns
new happiness, I can't say what.

Kinzua

*— in the Mohawk country of northwestern Pennsylvania
on the eve of construction of Seven Nations Casino*

The ground is wet and cold
where we abandon ourselves
to Alice Cooper & the Scorpions and set the tents
& central firepit circled by stones; we bring
the good knife from the Subaru's side-door compartment
& 2 days food, tarps, wine, & bread;
      breeze sifts through pine,
 I adjust the screen over the fire, brew the Yukon
   fine-grind, and roll a celebratory & elegiac
    joint while late frost

begins its sweat-melt under the Aries sun
 and something gray & unlabeled by clouds: sky
opens at the edge of the water;
  skunk cabbage switchblades
   release their horrible sweet smell.

     Sharp smoke
draws wavy lines around our space so we don't
  see the bobcat slip over the berm & climb the ridge

    accompanied by ghosts tamping messages
       deeper into the bulldozed trails;
we're fireside, early,
    solemn & exhilarated
     up here in the last of it.

Camping on the Hudson

Don't come up
you'll get lost
a voice said

Spring is rinsing the old rail towns
and floating barges clean as wet onyx

I'm daydreaming up here
You can't be seen, the white pines are so tall;
Lenape estuary
                 older than the Etruscans
& their fishing boat prayers
    older than the western arm of the Susquehanna
                    now buried under the shale fields

I walk the banks as if they were mine, magnified
versions of the small rivers of home

Don't thank God
thank Pete Seeger
the voice said

The metal-green waters wide & sea-like

Ducks cruise a quiet inlet
a mile square   *They used to be scared of sailing up here*

alone at night   *The cats wailed & wailed*

Last night my fire made my eyes smart,
   the wood was too wet   I was shaking
   when I found the paw print & scruff of fur in the bushes

The screeches even rattled Henry Hudson

Marten, lynx, polecat—
at home we call them all bobcat,
               not minding the difference

Ships came up through the Narrows
and busted their hulls on the jagged edges

The yowling never stopped all night
They camped close to the water, thinking
the big cats wouldn't come down to drink

The best views are far from everything
Poor people never get to live there

Before I went to sleep I doused my fire
and looked into the dark   Far away the Northern Lights'

siphons & scarlet wheels
sculpt themselves, throw off shapes
into the eyes of their beholder
whose face they mimic & imitate

& shift again to cat eyes &
now my fire-ring's
topaz & saffron stars

The Water Carriers

Sets of eyes—owls, stars—might notice
me following my father climbing the grade
up past the carwash & horse farm, through the ghost-
woods & Daugherty's Grove, *daughter*, I thought,
wanting the doll whose robe of ruby comets
once fluttered on the carnival stage.
I pass the ancient grandchild
asleep with a shotgun across her lap, sitting guard
to the southern curve of the dome,
Mohawk lookout dirt-dark under the sliver moon.
Perfect half-dome mowed by cow grazing all day
shadowblack mole-head alert into the night.
See him click the flashlight
on, see the slit in the ground where I lay with a boy
in the grass. Loose row of stones in the damp.
My father stares into the mound
the way he studies the glowing
dials of his machine
down in the cellar, kneeling
before it, writing words & numbers on little cards.
Loose row of stones, damp weeds
one reads water by
at the base of the dome. Bubbling spring
thrums to the surface. This is how
you know you're in a sacred place, he says.
Old burial mound, now called
Roundtop, hid under the half-lives
of a child's playfield.
                              —Father
opens a scratched sheet of aluminum door,

a slab of earth lifts to me,
I am eating it through my skin;
light-beam points down & in:
down the layers, grass, dirt, rocks, cinder, clay,
down to the round gray eye
of old water,
needled down
through the cold mineral vaults,
old water refreshing itself,
it's doing it right now
concentric circles swathing themselves
on its dense thin fields
washing themselves
under starlight & moonfall.
The murmuring
my father slid into &
through, how long
has he been gone?

Mohawk & Shawnee walked the 32 miles
the winding scout-path
to & from the Three Rivers
& under that long trail
one big gravel-bed of water.
—Giant aquifer—
under Roundtop
its guardian eye.
Father's water machine was the size
of a giant Philco, or UNIVAC 1130 computer
wide as a pick-up bed & braced & duct-
taped to copper sheets lining the wall.
An invention
no government or patent,
no Q clearance records;
designed to link the dome's
hidden water
to bigger waters.
It could predict storms & fair stretches,

inches of rainfall, high winds,
cloud density, anything we could
watch & see. He gauged
trade winds & studied
all the known universes: ancient,
Copernican, Galilean, Einstein
& beyond; he called them
stations, those men, wild
outposts to the atmospheres.
Followers all, creatures
in the dark, all of us,
he said loading boxes into his truck for the stranded
during the Great Snow of 1951.
Our brains are too small, he said
hooking chains onto the tires.
The Dodge shrank to a black dot
in the wind-bitten drifts
and when he came home
he ate & went down to the cellar.
Its dials & wires were so bright
the closer I got the smaller I was,
my grade-school glasses flared

through little glass windows
onto cities of wires & latitudes.
The blinking scarlet discs
were portals that shifted like phases of the moon,
he said, and they could read
farther liquid worlds,
water pockets & vapors
alive & capable of
moving in our direction.
My father said we could draw on them like wells.
He said, "I've left this for you."
Earth was smart and he would follow its lead.

I mind-walked
& my mouth watered for the fiery spirals at the edges.
In the old cellar
my spider shined under her work-
bench bulb and glinted thumbnail on & off mirrors
from circular saws & files. She stopped spitting
her thread, held one leg up in front of her head,
furred receptors zeroing in on me & all the light
in the room & up through the window.
I sat, wondering.

When he was 80 & in a hurry
Dad nailed a junkyard storm door
to the ceiling of his cellar
and the week we sold the house the potential
buyers, shy & hopeful, in love with the gardens & views
politely asked, "What's with the door?"
"It's a door to the stars," I said.
Everyone laughed. High over the roof
the invisible unsteady
vibrated, above & beyond a simple window
& equally homely
burial mound. Underground
here to there
the aquifer is saturating
the mole trails & under-girders
of plowed fields under the snows.

A Pittsburgh Novel

Hot pins of light crowning the avenue lamps shine up into Space, so I mind-walk to the walls at the ends without ends where comets shimmer like eyelashes of snow-deer. Last night a bus tumbled down a hillside into the river and all survived. Upstairs I conceived the old-fashioned way: I lay down with a man. I'm home alone polishing a mirror that reflects the roses from a sun-shot angle, & the wall lined with shells in honor of every war & mill dead I've counted. No diary. The facts of my daily existence bore me. It's the street coming into the house, rolling in on its blonde bricks & faceted cinders, delivering a dozen more names for wine, for water.

Clare of Shamokin

Traceries of her hand touching the storefront of ruby-glass goblets
where the lady gave us scraps of lace; before I held her
vet school hand, her newlywed then her women's shelter hand.

In her kitchen I peeled tomatoes while she cooked her spaetzle
& greens, cherry-stones on the grill and we drank;
then some new man who could melt her like butter. And last year

all the bills & blood tests piled up on her good pine desk.
The thruway's a good place to wail down the exit to her.
They're laying her out in one of her flowerchild dresses, thinking

her best of times. But it's a black & white scene, no music,
I take the ramp slow, arc lights turning like diamonds—

her one square stone, one round—and I am radically
asymmetrical before the fact of one more woman dead before 50.

The Gem Cutter

Someone upstairs is filling a kettle, faucet needs a washer—
stare at stones long enough you start hearing everything,
hazard of the trade. I dug these myself from a Catskill creek,
set them in gold & suddenly they're torches from the dead.
Ladies of London grew tired of Blackout, they wanted fire at their throats.
Chinese specimens hold drops of water who knows how old.
Romans loved rock crystals so much they carried them
in hottest summer—the ice that never melts.

Blade, slice down the edge like a song, like setting the table for the cake.

The Silver Tray

Backlit by the 40-foot
     white pine & tiered rock garden
  she planted 7 shades of blue

she walked slowly down the side-yard
     she called "lawn" when it was freshly cut
    summer mornings like this one
       in her gauze
blouse & gold sandals, graceful, balancing
     the good glass pitcher of crushed lemons
     sugar & ice, six or seven glasses
     wafer-cookies, floating,

the bluejay's funeral nearing its conclusion,
  we placed sticks at his head facing West.
    I'd cried when the priest scared me with the melting condemned

deep under the crust
  & Level Green's
     fields were cracked open with drought.

"Honey, there's no hell down there," she said brushing my hair.

"All of Level Green is built on water, an aquifer, the size of
  Rhode Island State."

    There is a special place for birds when they die.
    While they are being buried, by children or weather,
    there are other birds close by, she said, "like mourners."

Up in the pine
       they catch the silver glinting

               She is

carrying a funeral repast to a half dozen children

crossing the lawn

as if it were the meadow under Half Dome

or the Roosevelt lawns of Hyde Park

                   bearing the silver-plated tray
                   stored above a 3-step stool
                   placed before the tall cupboard
                   reached for, taken down,
                   removed from its plastic sheath
                   for deaths & birthdays.

We place marigolds & a clutch of her best white ruffled petunias

on the mound and say goodbyes. She is bending to slide the tray

onto a table and as it
               descends it catches

          sun and suddenly
                  on its underside
             I see a light-shadow

        that rotates & tilts
                  onto the grass
                      a white

disc, quivering there
    a silver-white oval
           lighting my mother's feet

I know are brown
from July's weeding & watering & walking us
to the store, playground, our friends' parties

but now her feet are white
          her gold sandals
           gone platinum

              and the grass

              is cast white

              under a second sun

              or moon turning the grass into

a circle
so bright I see single blades
free, tangled, spiraled, clumped—
            Tray clanks table—
               gone.

Now my mother stands free, left arm
  nursing her tight lower back,
           we circle her & lift our glasses,
      & drink & I cry
         for more before thanking her
         & clutching her, rubbing my face
         into her

as she was.

The Bowl

I saw under water between two rocks a small round bowl made of clear ice, interior concave smoothed, reflecting morning. Where the bowl came from and how it wedged itself here, who could feed from it, perfect for chilling fruit in July, for icing coffee with a dollop of sugared snow, I don't know. But the someone that might pluck it out of the water and set it over there on the flat rock, or carve it into spoons for a meal on that table, has left it here, under a thin membrane of water, preserving its fine shape & crystals. Rather not ask or disturb this instrument, place-mark, or lens I might lift to read the water books.

IV.
In an Ancient Garden

GIACOMO LEOPARDI

from To the Broom Flowers of Pompeii

On the dry back
of destroyer Vesuvius,
flower that blooms & scatters your lonely
twigs & bushes over the lava fields,

lover of sad places
where snakes nest & twist in the sun,
eighteen hundred years have passed
since the people & place

disappeared, crushed by fire.
At night in secret,
through empty theatres, deformed temples
& broken houses
where bats hide their young

the glow of the deathly lava
hurries like an insane torch
circling blackly through empty palaces
and from a distance
saturates the dead crimson

and stains everything in its path.
Ignoring us

& the ages we call ancient
Nature stays green all the time

moving ahead on a road so long
it seems to stand still.
Meanwhile, empires fall,

races & languages die.
Nature doesn't see this:
and humans still talk about eternity.
And you, flower,
gracing this bare place

with your slow brushes of scent,
you'll fall too,
you'll bend your lovely head
under your own mortal burden
without struggling.

In an Ancient Garden

Long before it enters
the pumice-filter of the aqueducts

the water invited lovers walking
into it believing their bodies

sanctify it & it them.
Animals birthed in it, trees fell into it

& released their casings to its blade-white
stillness, cloud-

shadows darkened
its lanes of dragonfly & trout.

Now a girl is lifting buckets
to fill a tank on one side of a garden wall.

A simple pipe threads the stone to
the other side so the trills

& beads slip down the silky panel
and into the head of an open-mouthed clay lion

guiding the liquid through its teeth
before a table heavy with figs & wine,

apricots & bread. A host of
arms & shoulders relax and reach

for that fresh water.
The tank holds a half-evening's supply so that

before the blue drape of night
falls, the girl lifts another three or four buckets

and she re-fills, listening
for the ahs & laughter on the other side.

For Aaron Sheon

"Tiny hatches, if you make enough of them, make

an entire etching move," you told us while we smoked

in the lit cave of your Tuesday 1-2:15. We scratched

our pens: dance & film posters, flyers to end the war.

In our famous jeans we slouched before your podium & slides weaving

the movements & the solo trips.

"He was lonely." "She had no patron."

"Scale extends us & reins us in," you said of the strange Piranesis.

"Find the heart of a city by stepping in."

My alleys & arcades pressed onto the copperplate of my 20-year-old brain

fusing its hemispheres.   I hitched to Colmar and found

the Isenheim Altarpiece, figures on the old panels aflame, then turned

my back on all religions because you'd shown us Goya's firing squad

& Daumier's gutters where people looked for water.

"Movement in a painting is important as Dante."

I've looked for Dante's houses, cafés, notebooks, & horse-stalls, & someone

always says   *Oh, you mean The Poet.*

"The body doesn't make sense by itself," you said, pointing the red-tip

wand at the chalky nudes of Ingres. If I am lonely

in any town whose museum

treasures its one Whistler or Bonnard, I stand before the image

hear your voice; my eyes

un-scroll, I lift

again like a hinge.

January Work

Bright night, inside & out,
desk lamp & moon-on-cement,
owl in spruce in 8-second
intervals, days are flying,
slips of paper list and scrawl,
projects worry the weeks, clocks
slide numbers down into the accumulating
past, how much can anyone do
in 1 day, 1 night: bits of thinking
like smoking chimneys keeping the street's
airspace warm so the rhododendrons
are forming thumb-size buds.
Everyone I know is looking for a job or
working 2; 3 if you count hauling
garbagesundrieslaundryfood
extended or nuclear family,
brushing animals, chopping ice
from bird baths so birds can actually
drink, rinsing a glass after you use it, wiping,
sweeping, the avalanche of housewifery.
What ladies' maids & only-wives used to do
to keep their charges clean & pressed & on-the-
wheel, you—gendered or
not—enact for your infantgranniesweetheartorboo.
In the middle of my peace the owl calls:
bold intervals
measuring the breadth
of my own labor
in the vast.

I Take My Mother to See the Rothko Panels, 2007

—(& she recites from Polish folklore)

Her eyes are adjusting
  like heat-sensors on low
in the dim gallery.

It's all touch; she leads,
her thin arm steers down, four steps,

another ten to the soft banquette, but we say bench
  & laugh at the old joke: her mother after a social call:
  "And what did she give you?" (it was the Depression:
  coffee, a roll?) "A bench to put my ass on."

We find ourselves
          in a dark room warm with paint, cool with stone.

That house was so reliable—Oh
he must have painted these at night.

In that house when you said goodnight you said
"Sleep red, sleep white," depending
on where you slept: the fire room, the white room.

These look more like stains than paint.
We had soot for conservation,
soon as the roof tiles
wore out on one side
we turned them over & nailed them back down.

64

Her mother's house on the banks of the Vistula
was bordered with willows & firs,
their greens brushed by weather.

She pulls us to breath-distance of the canvas
   so close we wash ourselves down
   in crimson & sienna, Rothko's Pompeii.
          He spiked his commission for the grand restaurant
  with "something that will ruin the appetite
               of every son-of-a-bitch who ever eats in that room."

We find ourselves in a room beamed by fire & stars.
   He must have painted these at night
         to get the maroons & oranges this warm.

During windstorms we thought the house walked,
It swayed like it was on springs,
bending in the winds & then
it came back to its original position.

  In a dark room beamed by fire & stars
    My grandfather stepped up onto the ladder—

he used cross-bars & sealed the beams
with forest moss, & later, wool.
Even the attic slats were shaped like sunbeams.

In the white room they had religious
pictures painted on glass.
He carved the sun
& the rosette, a star, up near the roof.

Baggage

I am moaning to Jerry I lost my Filofax fat blue overstuffed last seen Murray
Avenue Silk Pagoda lunch they don't have it never saw it; drive-thru bank
I dropped my coffee had to open the car door maybe it fell through the
grate, should I call the city and go underground. "You're crying about an
ADDRESS BOOK??" [Snorting.] I drop my voice like a drone. "My parents
gave it to me, a gift for my MFA, I had recipes, hotels, people, you know,
I don't know when I'll see them again but, stuff I'll never find." He starts:
"I lost an entire half no about a third no a sixth of a MANUSCRIPT, 13
poems on a train. Those 13 were brand new you don't know what I had to
do go through to get those what it was like I was buying cheap typewriters
Americans left behind after the War, repairing selling typewriters to try to
make a living in Paris after the War it was the Fifties how could I make a
living: enough to pay the landlord enough to buy Pernod & soda for the maid.
[Heh.] It was so beautiful you can't imagine. Everything was dove-grey one
of my favorite colors, sax keys, my pencils, of course the river, and the water
matched the benches, exactly, the lamps, her eyes, her liquid earrings. Those
trains I could sit there for hours screening my poems like little movies, I
could ride for days, the fields in the rain, that couchette so clear to me. Stop
thinking. Have you been sleeping? What's the smallest place you've ever
made love?" "Diving board," I say; he laughs. "Are you suffering? Isn't it
good to lose a little baggage?"

66

Rege Is Calling from Tuolumne Meadow

Six weeks out from the white-on-white cube

*

of ICU & emergency 6-bypass, (micro-twinge behind shoulder
while on treadmill),

*

he's the wiry smart one, cardio-science lab & astronomy one, sipping
from his flask

*

new boots already molded to his feet, hiker's luck, & skill: exactly calibrate
the flexible arches over the low boulders,

*

stretch like a cat & take it easy. "I think we should do the genealogy DNA
swab thing when you get back," I say,

*

restless to finally know the Sicilian part, & the Polish farming & insane wine-
grape-growing-in-the-shadows-of-steel-mills

*

part. Who were these people? "We already know Mom's an alien," he says,
listing the fashion shows she lives for.

*

We don't want to know the Argentina part, fearing among the hordes of
Vollmers down there a shameful Reich connection.

*

We weren't born then, are being born, still, this July morning it is 11:45 on
my porch, 8:45 on the Range of Light

*

"John Muir should be on Rushmore," I say. "But he'd hate anybody cutting
rock face,"

*

Rege says, signing off, "Love you; I'm off to leave no trace."

Camping on the Youghiogheny

Rocks in human-like shapes lift their knees

in the shallows, getting a taste of lunar light

and the dead file past on the left bank, one or two

leaving traces.   *Howl like a wolf,*
I command my stick & point at the moon.

The sky simplifies itself
to a pale gray swath tinted blue

while the river
twists below & above
the Mason Dixon Line

all the way to McKeesport & Great Valley of Brownfields & down south-
east again into the whitewater we worship at like a font

with our pride & fear, by which we, the president said,
[out of context]

"cling to [our] guns & religion"

and he was right.

Defacements line the phone poles—
spray-painted white-faced/big-lipped/
[they want him dead]

within eye-range of Fallingwater
>   where Wright brushed patented Cherokee Red paint onto

his pipeways & gutters, the rims of fireplaces & windows.   When my

brothers water-proofed our gates, pipes,

jungle-gym & handlebars they used Rustoleum

sparingly, as if it were ground from

>   pigments brought from Florence where our father once stood sketching

his version of a stronger Duomo rooftop.   Wright's project

required a special exit off the Turnpike

for his break-through client Edgar Kaufmann, & Edgar Jr's salons
>   of New York School
>   country weekends in the Laurels—

>   Edgar Jr. still closeted by tour guides whose script reads:
>   "He was scholarly."

A hawk's short flight to the Yough

>   whose death-trap water-knots

have claimed drunks, kayakers, lovers, and billions of fragments

of starlight. Now you see them now

they're pinched away & down & in

below my rock-ledge

in the thrashing. The shelf is slippery with Spring's

slush pushing gravel, grit, & splinters of shale

                    off its edge into holes
that thrust like geysers

from side-tipped emerald vases

ejecting runways for meadow-larks.

The lower Yough drags its sleeves
                          along the thin creeks
of sad Star Junction
          where Baci & Dziadzi's company house floorboards

once split & a child nearly slipped down
                              into the slime yellow waters.

Turn back,
          east of the mill look up
to Paule's Lookout
              where couples sipping Manhattans,
                  the women wearing rhinestones big as grapes,

gazed through picture windows

              down to the massive curve
                      to the juncture.

After Pavese's "Grappa in September"

No laziness like mine, little crystal cup,
tomatoes canned, late basil crushed to pesto.
Nothing better than 95 degrees in the shade.
People like us don't sweat in the heat because we work.
The sun finds a place on our skin and has no need to make it shine.

Night at Bosco

After the vino vecchia & circle of dear friends—
goodnight, & the call of the Athena owl sent me
toward sleep, but not before a strange sadness floated
at the edge of my room, a red rim or ledge I lingered near
as I had that morning at Selinunte, city of the dead
where I said goodbye to you, again,

from a wide balustrade near a quarry of rocks
waiting, 1,500 years later—to be set into the old city's streets. Then
Mary pointed to the thin silver-gray line
of stones leading downward & under the city
into the hidden streets where cisterns still hold cool water.

Notes

"On the Tarmac at Dover Air Force Base" is for the memory of Daniel Anderson: poet, friend, student, and Loyal Iroquois, who served in both Operation Just Cause (Panama) and Operation Desert Storm.

"A Reckoning" is for journalist Bill Heltzel, and for Maxine Kumin.

"Trees at Night" is for Norm and Karen Scanlon.

"Entering" is for the painter and installation artist Vera Manzi-Schacht.

"Camping on the Hudson" includes a variation on a phrase from Haruki Murakami's story "UFO in Kushiro," from *After the Quake*, Knopf 2002.

"The Water Carriers" is for my brothers, Regis and Robert; and for Ed Gevaudan, Beverly McWilliams, and Michael "Skip" Skvarla—Level Green Royalty, all. I am also indebted to the karst geologist Ira Sasowsky for conversations about aquifers in the Eastern United States.

"In an Ancient Garden" is for Colleen Randall.

"I Take My Mother to See the Rothko Panels, 2007" is for Mihaela Moscaliuc.

"After Pavese's 'Grappa in September'" quotes in its final line a sentence from Davide Lajolo's excellent biography of Cesare Pavese, *An Absurd Vice*, translated by Mario and Mark Pietralunga, New Directions 1983.

The Giovanni Pascoli and Giacomo Leopardi versions are mine.

Judith Vollmer's previous collections have received the Brittingham, the Center for Book Arts, and the Cleveland State publication prizes. She is the recipient of fellowships from the National Endowment for the Arts and the Pennsylvania Council on the Arts. Her essays and reviews are included in *The Cambridge Companion to Baudelaire* and elsewhere. She teaches at the University of Pittsburgh at Greensburg and in the Drew University MFA Program in Poetry and Poetry in Translation, and is a founding editor of the literary journal *5 AM.*

The Autumn House Poetry Series
Michael Simms, General Editor

• Winner of the annual Autumn House Poetry Prize

The Autumn House Poetry Series Continued

• Winner of the annual Autumn House Poetry Prize

Colophon

Cover and Text Design by Rebecca King

Author Photo © 2011 by Ann Begler

Title font: Gentium
Text font: Minion Pro

Printed by McNaughton-Gunn on 55# Natural Offset.

Cover Art by Sonia Delaunay, French, b. 1885 - d. 1979
Untitled, etching in four colors, 9 13/16 x 6 1/4 in.
Carnegie Museum of Art, Pittsburgh
Gift of Mr. and Mrs. Leon Anthony Arkus
Photograph © 2011 Carnegie Museum of Art, Pittsburgh

Sonia Delaunay (1885-1979), born Sarah Stern in Ukraine into a Jewish working class family, emigrated to Paris and Portugal where, before and during World War I, she made paintings that only recently have received their due as prefiguring Abstract Expressionism's arrival many decades later. In addition to her dazzling color work on canvas, Delaunay is a master of seemingly hastily sketched geometric forms—like those in the cover graphic, "Untitled," etching in four colors. Her hatches, grids, slashes, and spheres, suggesting cities, ruins, animals, and hauntingly etched fields, exemplify the iconic design sense that Delaunay also used in work on cloth in order to support her family, designing opera costumes, high fashion, and household textiles.

—Judith Vollmer